St. Francis
and His Feathered Friends

Anne E. Neuberger

Our Sunday Visitor Publishing Division
Our Sunday Visitor, Inc.
Huntington, Indiana 46750

Our Sunday Visitor Publishing Division
Our Sunday Visitor, Inc.
200 Noll Plaza
Huntington, IN 46750

ISBN: 1-931709-09-2 (Inventory No. R9)

Cover and interior design by Rebecca J. Heaston
Cover and text illustrations by Tessie J. Bundick

PRINTED IN THE UNITED STATES OF AMERICA

To Clare, Richie, and Jeannie and Dick Podvin,
Franciscans all!
A.E.N.

To all my young friends in Glacier National Park.
T.J.B.

A NOTE TO PARENTS AND TEACHERS

St. Francis of Assisi (1182-1226) is one of the best-known and most beloved historical figures. Despite his reputation for simplicity, his story is complex, revealing a man whose spirituality presents many challenges to us.

He was a pampered child and a rich young man with little direction in life. Illness and a series of diverse experiences caused him to do an about-face. Suddenly, he saw that his God was beckoning him in a totally new direction. Francis gave up his riches, helped the poor, and served the sick. He slept on the ground and begged for his food, embracing poverty.

His legacy to us is many-faceted: he represents the tremendous joy and freedom obtained only by giving oneself totally to God; his example can pose serious confrontations to the Church or society of any era; he teaches what a radical commitment to material poverty looks like, as well as a vision of a radical commitment to nonviolence; his love for Jesus was so deep that he received the stigmata, the physical signs of Jesus' passion, a discomforting fact to many observers.

There is much material in Francis' life for adults to ponder and emulate. Still, he is so profoundly important that our children should be introduced to him at an early age.

For this, we turn to stories of yet another facet of Francis' spirituality: his well-lived belief that all things — inanimate, animal, and human — reflect our Creator's love. For this reason, everything deserves reverence and wonder. Because children, too, are still close to reverence and wonder for God's creation, they can embrace Francis as their own. As they get older, their identification with him can lead them to his more complicated teachings.

Through stories, the past becomes present once again. So, through them, St. Francis can come to live in our children's imaginations. There he can teach his messages of divine love, creation as a reflection of that love, and how to live out the Gospel.

And remember, stories may enter into us through our minds, but they settle in our hearts.

May this story bring Francis into the hearts of your children.

—A.E.N.

The small man known as Brother Francis walked down a path in his brown robe. His feet were bare and dusty, but his heart was full of God's love.

And how he delighted in singing about this! He could sing in both Italian and French, and he sang loudly. Francis also loved to roam about from town to town, telling everyone and everything he met about God and His gifts to us.

One day he and Brother Leo and Brother James followed a winding path in a valley. All around them were curling vines, wild flowers, and the greens and silvers of the olive trees. Francis was singing to all of it.

As they rounded a bend, he stopped singing and stood very still. Ahead of them was a vast meadow. “Look!” Francis cried with delight. “My sisters, the birds!”

And indeed, the meadow was filled with birds of all kinds! There were orange-throated finches, long-tailed magpies, sharp-eyed crows and their cousins, the rooks. There were gentle doves, humble larks, wood pigeons, and fork-tailed swallows. Some perched in trees, and many more covered the ground. But strangely, they were all silent.

"It's as if they are waiting for you, Brother Francis," Brother Leo whispered very softly.

But Francis was anything but quiet. He whooped and dashed towards the meadow. Still, not a bird moved, not a feather ruffled.

"Even the magpies are still!" Brother James marveled.

Francis ran to them, but the birds on the ground simply looked up at him. Those in trees fluttered down, settling among the other birds. Francis laughed in delight.

"May the Lord be with you, my little sisters!" Francis said. "Now pay close attention, for I have much to tell you."

The birds tilted their heads to listen.

"How beautifully dressed you are! And how free your wings make you! You have the whole sky to frolic in! Our Creator has given you streams to drink from, and trees to nest in, and food all over! How God must love you! You should always and everywhere sing your songs of praise to your Maker!"

The birds were joyful. They flapped their wings. They stretched out their necks, wanting to see this brother of theirs. Some opened and closed their beaks — but still, all were silent. There was not a chirp, a cheep, a caw, or a squawk.

Francis began to walk among them. His rough robe brushed against some of them, but the birds held still. Making a sign of the cross over the birds, Francis blessed them. "Now fly, my little sisters," Francis said, "and praise our God with your songs!"

With a rush of wings, the crowd of birds rose into the air. Their songs filled the countryside as they flew off, some to the north, others to the south, to the west, and to the east.

Brother Leo shouted, "They are flying in the shape of Jesus' cross, reaching in all directions!"

As he gazed after them, Brother Francis wondered, "Why haven't I spoken to my little sisters before? From now on, I'll talk with all of God's creatures. They should learn about God's love for them, too."

When they reached the town of Alviano, it was early evening. Children came running and skipping to greet them, waving branches and shouting. Someone rushed to ring the church bell to announce that Francis had come. Doors slammed as people hurried to the market square to surround him.

Now Francis was not a tall man, and he was soon lost in the crowd. So he climbed up some steps as the others gathered around. Above them all in the evening sky, a flock of swallows was wheeling, gliding, looping, and soaring. All the while, they twittered loudly to one another.

None of the people noticed the birds, for they were calling their children to them and jostling their way closer to the steps. Eager to hear Brother Francis, the townspeople settled the babies and became silent themselves.

"May the Lord be with you —" began Francis.

No one could hear him for all the chatter of the swallows. Francis chuckled a little and called out to his feathered friends, "My Sister Swallows! It's my turn to speak now! You've said enough already. Listen to God's word! Stay still until I'm finished!"

The birds stopped their twirling flights and settled down quickly on the surrounding rooftops. The astonished people looked at one another. Smiling, Francis began to speak. The birds remained absolutely silent until he finished.

Another day, as Francis ambled down the road, he met a boy swinging a cage full of frightened turtledoves. The boy was going to the market to sell the birds.

Now Francis loved all of God's creatures. He saw them as part of his family, and treated them politely. Francis did not like seeing his family in a cage!

Still, he was kind to the child. "My good boy," he said, "please give me those doves."

The boy looked at the doves huddling in the cage. He had worked hard to catch them, and he wanted the money he would get for them.

"These doves have done nothing wrong. If you sell them, someone cruel might buy them," Francis said.

The boy looked up into Francis' eyes. He handed the cage to Francis and then walked on.

Francis sat down and opened the cage. Bringing out each dove, he held it to his chest. Stroking their sand-colored feathers, he said softly, "My simple and innocent Sister Doves, why did you let yourselves be caught?"

The doves answered, "Hoo-hrrooo!"

A smile spread on Francis' face. As he stood up, all the doves fluttered to the ground around him. They strutted along with him as he picked up twigs and odd bits of straw. Then he sat down, his lap filled with his findings. The doves cocked their heads to watch as Francis slowly fashioned nests. Then he nestled the nests into trees and bushes.

"Now, settle in, my little sisters," he said, with a small stick still clinging to his robe.

Soon baby doves were peeking out of those nests. When the friars came outside, the doves flew down to perch on their shoulders or heads.

When Francis came outside, all the doves flocked to him.

"Hello, Sister Doves! How are the babies today?" Francis asked.

"Hoo-hrrooo!" they said.

"Good! Now go back to your work and I'll go on with mine," Francis said.

But not a dove moved.

"You won't leave without a blessing, will you?"

"Hoo-hrrooo!"

So Francis blessed the gentle doves, and they flew back to their nests.

As the years passed, Brother Francis became weak and sick. He still prayed each day. He still felt God's strong love. He still lived simply. And he still loved his sister birds.

Francis had always enjoyed visiting lonely places. There he could pray and listen for God's answers. Even when he was sick, he loved to be alone. One time, he stayed in a tiny hut high in the Italian hills. But he was not alone for long.

One day, a falcon flew down to the hut, perching on the windowsill with its strong, curved talons. Francis looked up into the bright eyes and hooked beak of this bird.

"Welcome!" Francis said. "You must have a nest nearby."

Bird and brother focused intense, sharp eyes at each other for a moment. "I think we understand each other," Francis said.

Each morning, Brother Francis tried to wake before the sun's light touched the hills. Despite feeling sick, he wanted to be up to talk to God.

His friend the falcon arrived then. She came to pray in her own way, by beating her powerful wings.

Brother Francis had no alarm clock. One morning, he overslept. The sun was inching its way up in the east when the falcon arrived. Perched on the windowsill, the bird could see Francis was still asleep. In a loud voice, the falcon called to Francis to awaken.

Francis opened one eye to see the falcon's powerful gaze. The bird squawked at him again. A laugh deep inside of Francis came tumbling out. "Good morning to you, my sister! I have no excuse for sleeping late with you around!" he said.

The falcon beat her wings. Francis laughed again. "Yes, you are right. It is time to pray."

One night, Francis was very ill. He tossed and turned, trying to get comfortable. He groaned and sighed in pain. Finally, as the morning star appeared, Francis was able to sleep peacefully.

The falcon was nearby but did not come to the windowsill. It wasn't until sunup that the falcon lighted on the window and called to Brother Francis.

When Francis awoke, he saw the falcon and the sunshine outside. "My kindhearted friend," he said to the bird, "you knew I needed some extra sleep today, didn't you?"

The falcon beat her wings.

Slowly sitting up, Francis grinned at the bird. "Yes, it is time to pray!"

As the sun's warming rays spread out across the hills, Brother Francis and his sister bird prayed together once again.

Ever since Francis was a little boy, he had watched the larks, humble birds in earthen-colored coats. They wore funny feather crowns on their heads. He enjoyed seeing flocks of them walking along the ground. And then his spirit would lift with them as they flew high into the sky, singing sweetly and joyously. "You sing the loveliest songs!" he rejoiced. All his life, Francis had loved larks.

But now, Francis was becoming weaker and weaker. Soon his humble body, in its earthen-colored robe, would die. Then his spirit could soar to be with the God who loved him.

As Francis lay dying, a cloud of larks gathered on a nearby roof. Then, flying in low circles so Francis could hear them, his beloved feathered friends began to sing. They sang sweetly and joyously, saying their farewells to the brother they so loved. They sang the loveliest songs.